FIELD HOCKEY: THE BEGINNER'S GUIDE

B&W Edition

By Cristopher Maloney

No matter what our greatness,
What degree, or why it came
The one through whom it surfaced
Is our coach by any other name

– *Cris Maloney*

To my late wife
Barbara Ruth Benowitz Maloney
for her love and support

CONTENTS

PREFACE

Field Hockey: The Beginner's Guide will help readers learn how to play and coach the great sport of field hockey.

In addition to an overview of the sport, packed with illustrations and photographs, this book includes exclusive and detailed coverage of the *Maloney Method™*. The genesis of the *Maloney Method* came from a presentation titled *Field Hockey: The First 30-Minutes* that I made at an International Olympic Committee *Olympic Solidarity* course held at the US Olympic Training Center in 1985. Since that time the *Maloney Method* has been used to train thousands of beginners in private lessons, recreation programs, and physical education classes.

Peer-to-peer teaching is a great way to expand the number of participants in a sport. This is easy to do with the *Maloney Method* because it provides teenagers with an easy to remember system they can use to teach their friends or younger children. Using the *Maloney Method*, for example, a girls' field hockey team can, in a single afternoon, teach the boys' soccer team how to play the game and have challenging opponents in their school ready to play in weekly scrimmages.

Anyone who becomes skilled in the *Maloney Method*, can use it to introduce field hockey to new players in as little as 30-minutes.

You Can Umpire Field Hockey

Earn about $50 per hour exercising and watching a great game. We made your first call easy. The course is online!

UmpireHockey.com/enroll

CHAPTER 1

THE GAME

Field hockey is a fun sport that began thousands of years ago. It is played outdoors on artificial and grass surfaces and is one of the most popular sports in the world for boys and girls, and men and women. A similar game, indoor hockey, is played indoors on hard surfaces.

Field hockey is played in recreational leagues, private clubs, schools, colleges, professional leagues, and at the Olympics. At the Olympics, 12 mens and 12 womens teams compete separately for medals.

Hundreds of countries have national teams that try to qualify for the Olympics.

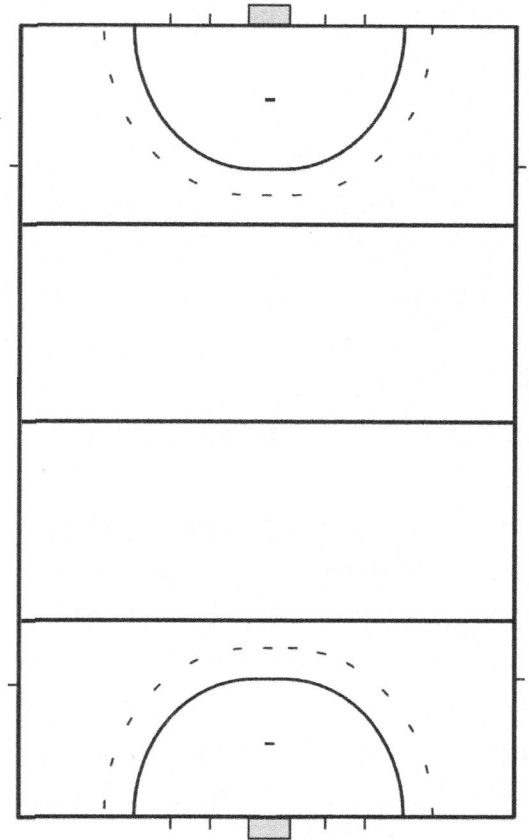

The field hockey competition surface is 100 yards long and 60 yards wide/91.44x54.86 meters. There is a scoring zone, called the circle, and goal at each end of the field.

The official version of indoor hockey is played on a hard surface, in a space a little larger than a basketball court. Four-inch tall aluminum or wooden barriers on the sidelines help keep the ball from going out-of-bounds. Like the outdoor game, there is a goal and scoring circle at each end of the court.

Other differences between indoor hockey and field hockey are that indoor players are not allowed to play the ball while kneeling or lying down, are not allowed to hit the ball, and, unless shooting, they may not lift the ball. In addition to the smaller court size, the goalmouth of indoor hockey goals is smaller than outdoor goals, as is the scoring zone. There are also fewer players from each team in the game – six indoor hockey players versus eleven field hockey players.

Despite those differences, an indoor hockey game, with 40 minutes of playing time, typically has more scores in less time than those seen in much longer field hockey games.

Field hockey for older teenagers and adults is played with eleven players per team, ten are called field players and one is the team's goalkeeper.

Most field hockey games last about an hour, with a short rest period halfway through. After the break, the teams change ends and attack the goal that they were previously defending. Two umpires officiate each contest and enforce the rules. When the teams switch ends, the umpires do not. This gives the attackers and defenders an equal amount of time with each umpire.

Each player, except for the goalkeeper, must only use their stick to play the ball. Only one side of the stick can be used to play the ball. Goalkeepers are allowed to play the ball with their body.

Players use a stick that is about three feet long. The longest a stick can be is 41.34 inches/105 centimeters. All sticks are designed in a very similar fashion. The top half of the stick is round, so it can be easily held. The bottom of the stick is flat on one side, round on the other, and curves into a hook at the end. It is against the rules for the ball to be played with the round side of the stick.

The ball is rock hard and a little bigger and heavier than a baseball. It is made of hard plastic and is hollow inside. Because the ball is so hard and can be moved with great velocity, field players wear protection over their shins and goalkeepers are heavily padded all over.

To win the game, one team must score more points than the other. To get points, a team must play the ball into the goal that the other team's goalkeeper is protecting. The winning team is the one that is most successful at getting the ball into their opponent's goal.

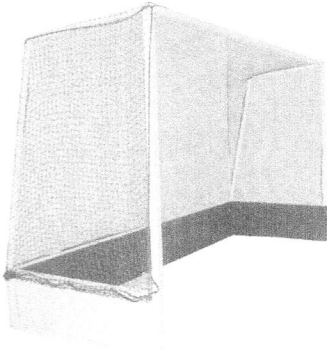

The official goal size for an outdoor game is 7 feet high by 12 feet wide/2.13x3.66 meters. The scoring area of the goal used for indoor games is about 25% smaller than that of an outdoor goal. The official size of an indoor hockey goal is 6.56 feet high by 9.84 feet wide/2x3 meters. The indoor and outdoor goals have backboards and sideboards that are 18 inches tall. Youth and recreational games often use very small goals.

Men's field hockey was introduced at the Olympic Games in 1908. The women's tournament was added in 1980. India dominated the Olympics from 1928 to 1964, winning the men's gold medal in seven out of eight Olympics. Pakistan has also been dominant, winning three gold and three silver medals between 1956 and 1984. In recent decades, the world's best teams have come from European countries and Australia.

In the meantime, teams from China, Japan, and Korea have made undeniably strong showings in international tournaments while India, Pakistan, and New Zealand are regularly among the top ten teams in the world rankings. In short, field hockey is truly a global sport.

The USA Men's National Team has competed in three Olympics – 1936*, 1984, and 1996 (all because the USA was the host nation). The USA Women's National Team competed in six Olympics – 1984*, 1988, 1996, 2008, 2012, and 2016. The USA Women's also qualified to play in the 1980 Olympic Games in Moscow but the USA boycotted those Games.

Bronze medalist

RECENT OLYMPIC MEDAL WINNERS

2016 Rio de Janeiro, Brazil		2012 London, England		2008 Beijing, China	
Men	*Women*	*Men*	*Women*	*Men*	*Women*
1. Argentina	1. Great Britain	1. Germany	1. Netherlands	1. Germany	1. Netherlands
2. Belgium	2. Netherlands	2. Netherlands	2. Argentina	2. Spain	2. China
3. Germany	3. Germany	3. Australia	3. Great Britain	3. Australia	3. Argentina

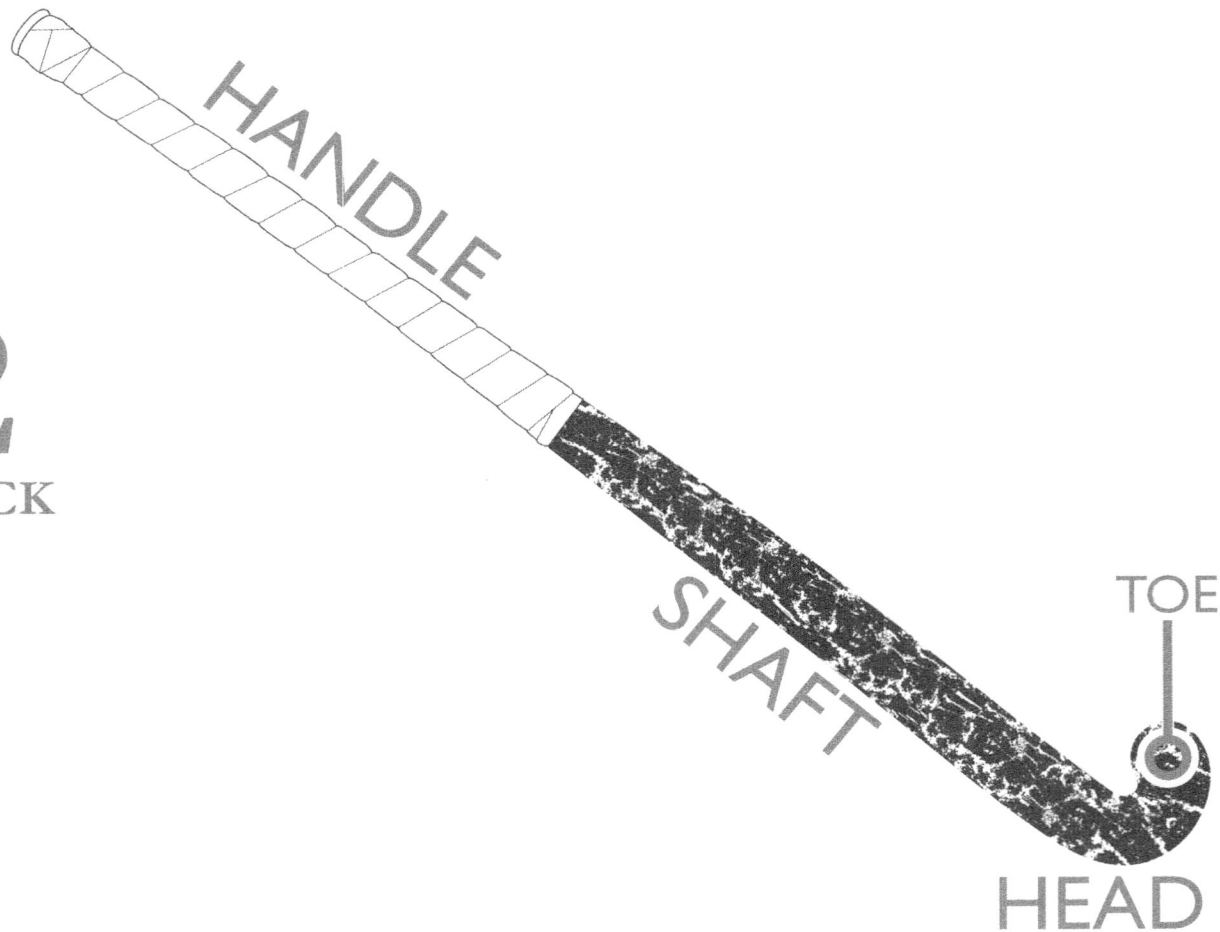

HANDLE

CHAPTER 2

THE STICK

TOE

SHAFT

HEAD

Field Hockey: The Beginner's Guide

There's a lot to be said about endurance, speed, footwork, wrist and shoulder strength, and game sense but, players have to have a stick to actually play the game. Before we learn about how players select a stick, let's go over the basic parts of the stick.

All sticks are designed for the ball to be played primarily on the right side of the body. This right-side design requirement makes it easier for right handers to master the hitting action. Left handers, however, have better initial ball control because the fine motor skills needed for fancy dribbling are performed by the left hand.

HANDLE: The top half of the stick is round, like a dowel. The players manage the stick using the handle.

SHAFT: About halfway down the stick, the handle begins to get wider and flatter. This part of the stick is called the shaft and is rarely touched by the players. As illustrated in the cross section (right), one side of the shaft is arched and the other side is flat. The side that is arched is called the round side of the stick. The other side is, unsurprisingly, called the flat side.

CROSS SECTION

The Stick

The round side and the flat side are connected by parts of the stick called the edges. The edges are not well defined. They are simply those parts of the stick where the flat and round sides come together.

IMPORTANT REMINDER: The ball is never allowed to be played with the round side of the stick.

TOE: The bottom of the stick is called the head. It curves to make a hook and ends in what is called the toe. The more advanced players become (right-side attacker, left-side midfielder, center defender, etc.), toe style might play a role in stick selection. For new players to the game, toe style just does not matter.

The width of the stick is not allowed to exceed two inches (51mm) at any point. If the stick doesn't easily pass through a metal stick ring, designed for umpires to use to check the width of sticks, the stick will not be allowed in the game. None of the manufacturers make sticks that are too wide, but some players wrap tape around their sticks and if they put on too many layers of tape, the stick will no longer pass through the stick ring.

Players can hit the ball at very high rates of speed. In fact, men can swing a field hockey stick at more than 100 miles per hour – a faster swing than found in any other sport.

According to ESPN Sports Science, the average swing speed of the men's field hockey stick is 103 miles per hour/165.76 kilometers per hour.

Field Hockey	103mph	Tennis (serve)	75mph
Golf	100mph	Cricket	67mph
Baseball	76mph	Ice Hockey	60mph

Like baseball bats, field hockey sticks range in price from $50 to $500. Just because a stick is expensive does not mean it is better for a beginner. As players gain more experience, they'll get more picky about minor differences between sticks – as well they should. These subtle differences are explored in detail in Chapter 3, Picking A Stick.

TIP: When athletes start playing field hockey, and they're not even sure they like the sport, try to borrow a stick or purchase one at a store that sells used equipment.

Sticks come in different lengths, any number of colors, and slightly different weights and shapes. All players, regardless of experience, should begin by focusing on getting a stick that is the correct length.

As mentioned, most players use a stick that is about 36 inches/91 centimeters in length. While there is no minimum length, the maximum length of a stick cannot exceed 41.34 inches/105 centimeters.

A combination of factors, such as arm length and upper body strength, make picking a stick that's a good length and weight unique to each player. The table below is from the Phoenix Field Hockey stick company. It is only meant to serve as a guide for selecting a stick's proper length. In fact, missing from the table are sizes in half-inch increments and most sticks are available in lengths such as 36.5". More selection information is provided in the next chapter.

PLAYER HEIGHT	STICK LENGTH	PLAYER HEIGHT	STICK LENGTH
Up to 4'4"	32"	5'5" – 5'9"	36"
4'4" – 4'7"	33"	5'10"– 6'2"	37"
4'8" – 5'0"	34"	6'3" – 6'8"	38"
5'1" – 5'4"	35"		

PHOENIX

CHAPTER 3

PICKING A STICK

Contributed by Phil Danaher,
Chief Engineering Officer
Phoenix Field Hockey

When athletes first start out playing field hockey, they normally will borrow a stick, or purchase the least expensive stick, whether new, or used, until they have decided to continue in the sport.

Rather than focusing on the underlying engineering, and even though field hockey sticks will range in price from about $50 to over $500, many players will make their purchase because of the colors and graphics used on a stick. The reasons above will not make a player better, or play more skillfully. Colors and graphics are enticing but, **it's what's inside that counts!**

The high priced sticks are made for the biggest, strongest, and most advanced skill-level players. They are typically the stiffest sticks.

Athletes will play much better with a stick that is the correct length, weight, head design, and flexibility for the surface they play on, their height, strength, and skill level of hitting and receiving.

The surface they play on will be impacted by the shape of the head and weight of the stick.

Different head shapes aid in different dribbling and flicking skills. Different weights aid in driving, dribbling, and throwing of the ball. The length of the stick will impact an athlete's ability to get low, and both the dribbling skills successfully utilized and club head speed when hitting. Most sticks weigh between 18 and 22 ounces/510-624 grams.

The stiffer the stick, the faster the ball will come off the head, but if proper technique is not used, it will go off faster in the wrong direction. A stick with a little flex will stay in contact with the ball longer and the player's aim will become more accurate as the body movement progresses through the skill.

The same results happen when receiving the ball. A very stiff stick will cause the ball to bounce off the stick much more than a stick with a small amount of flex.

The advantage of a stiff stick is with players of exceptional strength and skill. They can get the stiff sticks to bend and their hits are accurate and fast. The responsiveness when dribbling will also be higher and they receive the ball tight to the stick. These world-class athletes possess the skills and strength that make the most expensive (stiffer) sticks more worthwhile.

The length of the stick is determined by many factors, such as arm length, leg length, playing surface and the player's ability to stay low when performing skills.

NOTE: The guide used for the table in the previous chapter is for a stick with a full-sized head.

Given that the sticks are available in half-inch increments, you can see there is no exact stick length, or weight, that one can predict based on a player's height. Athletes will change stick lengths and weights as their body changes with strength and age.

Being comfortable with the stick an athlete buys will be the biggest advantage they can provide themselves. No one brand, model, color, or level of stiffness is right for everyone.

Understanding some of the unique design features we put into Phoenix field hockey sticks may also help athletes with their stick selection. For example, the inside wall of a Phoenix is thicker than a normal stick to provide both extra reinforcement and a wider hitting surface for backhand edge hits.

The diameter of the mid-shaft, just below the handle, has been widened by 4mm to provide both a larger surface area for the right hand when flicking, and more surface area to add strength in this transition part of the stick. And, the core of a Phoenix utilizes a patent pending design that provides unprecedented engineering.

Additional design features, detailed below, will help athletes refine their choices so they select the Phoenix that is perfect for their strength, playing skills, position, and the competition surfaces on which they are competing.

T–SERIES (Traditional Head)
The T–Series sticks have a traditional thickness head of 28mm across the center of the bulb (the thickest part of the head). T–Series sticks are designed for use on grass and field turf. Players who enjoy a heavier head and don't tend to throw the ball overhead will love this stick.

H–SERIES (Hybrid Head)

The H–Series sticks have a new thinner head than traditional sticks at 24.5mm across the center of the bulb. The inside wall is slightly larger to allow more consistent contact when using a backhand edge hit. The H–Series stick is designed for great success on all hockey surfaces. Strong hits, easy lifts, and a balanced head make this a great stick for both dribbling and driving of the ball. This is an outstanding stick for all areas of the field and styles of play.

K–SERIES (Goalkeeper)

These sticks have the look of the H or I series sticks, but are lighter through the mid-shaft area and more flexible to allow the ball to be caught and dropped by the goalkeeper. The head has the normal weight of a field stick, providing balance and support for the goalkeeper. These are 20% lighter than normal sticks.

I–SERIES (Indoor Head)

The I–Series of sticks are for Indoor hockey. They have varied amounts of flex for receiving the ball flat on the ground, but provide excellent power for flicks. The head is 16mm, providing a slightly thicker head than traditional indoor sticks to produce more control when dribbling and receiving hard passes.

HANDLE

Shock reducing
foam filling

MID SHAFT

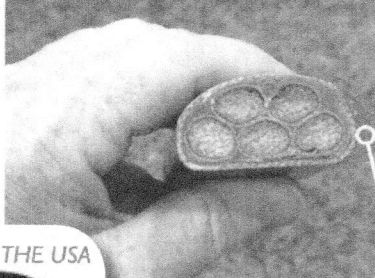

Reinforced
Back-Hand Edge

MADE IN THE USA

PHOENIX

LOWER SHAFT

TOE & HEAD

Picking a Stick

CHAPTER 4
THE UNIFORM

The uniforms worn by field hockey teams are most similar to those worn in soccer, with one difference – many female field hockey players wear skirts or kilts instead of shorts.

When women first started playing field hockey in the late 1800's, they weren't allowed to wear pants, let alone shorts. They played field hockey in long skirts that reached the ground. Over time, the length of the skirts shortened. It was probably in the early 1960's when uniform skirts stopped reaching the knees. Only a hint of this "long" history remains. Now, players who aren't wearing shorts are wearing very short skirts with built in shorts – also known as skorts. Teams can play in a mix of shorts, skirts, skorts, and kilts if they are similar in color and don't create confusion.

Uniform tops have numbers, typically ranging from 00 to 99. That said, a team cannot have a player wearing zero (0) and another wearing double zero (00).

Goalkeepers and field players with goalkeeping privileges must wear a numbered shirt that is a different color from the

field players on both teams, but they can match the other goalkeeper.

Field players must wear knee socks that match their teammates.

All players need to wear shin guards and mouth guards, and appropriate shoes (to help prevent slipping).

SHIN GUARDS: Players have to protect their shins from the ball and opponents' sticks. Shin guards cover the lower legs from just above the shoes to just below the knees. There are two kinds of shin guards. One is called a sock guard and the padding is embedded within a sock. The other kind fits over the shin like an exoskeleton. This kind of shin guard is form-fitting and made of hard plastic. It is placed on top the shin and a knee sock is pulled over it, which holds it in place during competitions.

I like sock guards for pre-teens and young teenagers because one just tosses the whole thing in the wash after each use.

CHAPTER **5**
OTHER GEAR

MOUTH GUARDS: There are two type of mouth guards, bulky and super thin. They should be replaced every year to keep pace with changes in the size and alignment of the teeth and, typically, to maintain manufacturer's warranties and offers of insurance.

SHOES: I include shoes with other safety related products because without the right shoes, players can injure their ankles or knees, or even fall – endangering themselves and others.

COURT   CLEATS   TURF

COURT shoes, also known as flats, are the only acceptable type of athletic shoe for playing on hardwood/plastic. Flats can be worn outside on dry surfaces, but they are not ideal for grass.

Shoes with a handful of long protrusions, usually 7 per shoe, are commonly known as **CLEATS**. They are appropriate for grass and artificial surfaces configured with a dirt replacement, typically a crumb-rubber or organic filler, mixed with tiny granules of sand, commonly called field turf.

TURF shoes have "too-many-to-count" short protrusions that provide the traction players need to complete at top speed. They are appropriate for tightly-woven artificial surfaces that do not have a filler product between the fiber blades. These surfaces are known as water-based turfs because for high-level competitions they are soaked prior to the start of the game and during halftime. Neither flats nor cleats are appropriate for use on water-based surfaces.

Young children and pre-teens do not typically weigh enough and are typically not fast enough to gain any benefit from cleats or turf shoes unless the surface they are playing on is wet.

HINT: Before playing on wet grass, apply vegetable oil (or similar product) on the bottom of your cleats. The vegetable oil will keep mud and grass from sticking between the long protrusions.

RECOMMENDED OPTIONS
GLOVES: It's a really good idea to wear protective gloves, especially when playing the indoor game on hard surfaces. The gloves field hockey and indoor hockey players wear are padded to protect the back of the hand and fingers. The palm of the hand does not need padding. In fact, padding on the palm would diminish stick control.

Field Hockey: The Beginner's Guide

SAFETY MASKS (DEFENDING PENALTY CORNERS)

While optional, safety masks should be worn by each and *EVERY* defender of *EVERY* age on *EVERY* penalty corner (see chapter 8, "Penalty Plays" to learn about penalty corners). Even young players can hit the ball hard. The ball can rise directly from a miss hit or a deflection and it only takes one hit to the head to turn a young player off to the sport or, worse, cause an injury.

WHAT ABOUT GOGGLES?

Metals goggles are dangerous, especially to opponents, and should never be worn. Sports goggles with prescription lenses are available and allowed to be worn.

WHAT ABOUT HELMETS FOR FIELD PLAYERS?

The first thing you have to know is that no helmet, not even those worn by professional football players in the USA, prevent or even reduce the number of concussions athletes get or their severity. Therefore, don't buy a helmet if you think wearing one will reduce the likelihood of getting a concussion. The only thing helmets do on a regular basis is protect the wearer from soft tissue injuries. Regardless, the only head protection allowed to be worn by field players during open field play must be one made of soft material. Again, neither soft nor hard helmets prevent or reduce the severity of concussions.

CHAPTER 6
THE GOALKEEPER

There is one player who not only uses their stick to play the ball, but can also use their entire body– the goalkeeper.

The goalkeeper is heavily padded and is allowed to use their body to play the ball when they are inside the scoring zone, i.e. the circle, and when they are not restarting play.

Except in high schools in the USA, a team may remove the goalkeeper and play with all field players. Years ago, teams could play with a "kicking back" – a player with goalkeeping privileges who does not wear goalkeeping equipment but was allowed to kick the ball when it was in the circle. This was never allowed in high school games and is no longer legal at any level of the game.

Remember, goalkeepers only have special privileges while they, and the ball, are within the circle. Despite all these special privileges, not even goalkeepers are allowed to play the ball with the round side of their stick.

Goalkeepers and attackers often collide when both are

THROAT PROTECTION

RIGHT HAND PROTECTION

PELVIC PROTECTION

LEG GUARD

KICKER

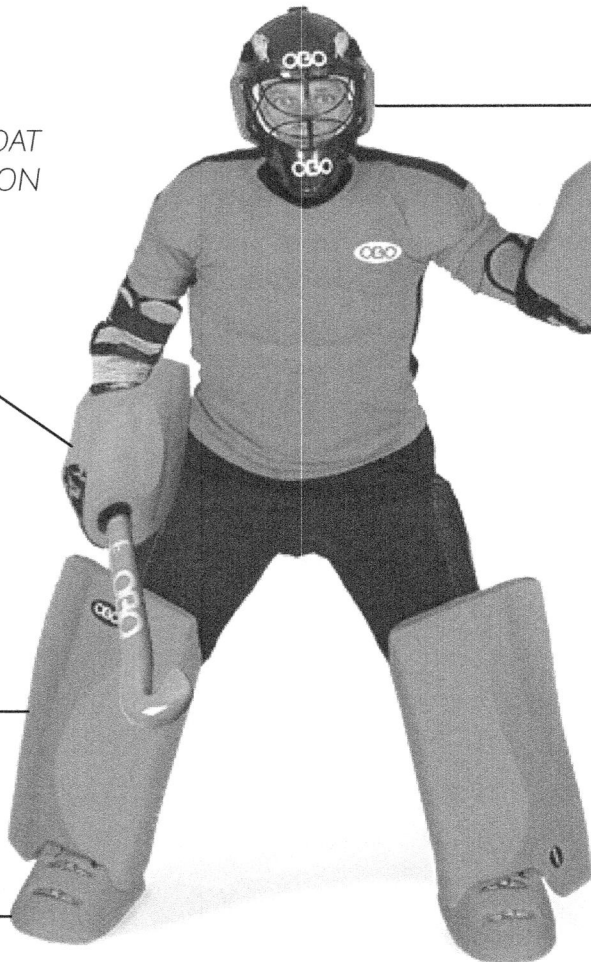

HEAD PROTECTION: HELMET AND FIXED FACEMASK

LEFT HAND PROTECTION

STERNUM, TORSO, ARM, ELBOW PROTECTION

HIP AND THIGH PROTECTION

Field Hockey: The Beginner's Guide

making legitimate plays for the ball. However, goalkeepers must not play in a reckless or dangerous manner just because they are wearing protective equipment.

Collisions between a goalkeeper and an attacker are typically tough calls for the umpire.

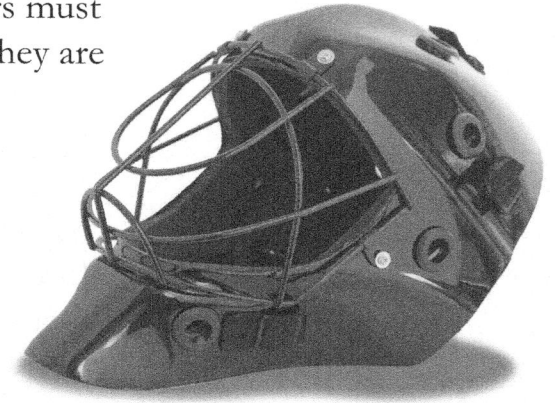

7
PLAYING RULES

It's not my intention to discuss every rule in detail but to provide a reasonable overview of the most important ones.

If you're interested in learning more, take my online rules course available on UmpireHockey.com. The *Rules of Hockey* and *Rules of Indoor Hockey* are available for free on the International Hockey Federation website (FIH.ch) and are required reading.

In the USA, there are three sets of rules governing outdoor competitions. They are the *Rules of Hockey*, the National Collegiate Athletic Association (NCAA) modifications to the *Rules of Hockey*, and the National Federation of State High School Associations (NFHS), which wrote its own set of rules and regulations.

The NCAA modifications are largely what would otherwise be known as tournament regulations and provide consistency across all college competitions for administration of games. The playing rules are not changed. For example, halftimes in NCAA games are required to be 10-minutes in length.

The NFHS wrote a complete set of rules and they're used to govern games between almost all high schools in the USA. While this rule set is also used to create administrative regulations, it also creates inconsistencies that make it difficult for coaches, players, umpires, and fans who move between high school games and those governed by the *Rules of Hockey*.

TEAM COMPOSITION: There are eleven players in the game for each team in the outdoor game. One of those players is almost always a goalkeeper. In indoor hockey, each team competes with six players, one of whom is usually a goalkeeper.

LENGTH OF GAME: Field hockey is played in 15-minute quarters. At the highest level of the game, this allows for commercial breaks for games that are televised. A 2-minute break is given between the first and second quarter, and the third and fourth quarter. A halftime break is never more than 10-minutes in length. These time periods are the same at nearly all levels of the game. Youth games might be played in 20- to 25-minute halves.

NOTE: Indoor hockey games consist of 10-minute quarters. An one-minute interval is given between the first and second quarter, and the third and fourth quarter. Halftime is three minutes in length.

SCORING: In field hockey, in order to score, two things must be true. One, a player on the attacking team has to have touched the ball while the ball is inside the circle. Two, the ball must go into the goal before it otherwise leaves the circle. In short, the attack has to score from within the circle. In field hockey, the circle ends 16 yards/14.63 meters away from the goal-line. In indoor hockey, the circle ends 9.84 yards/9 meters away from the goal-line.

NOTE: The shape of the circle is NOT a circle. It most closely resembles a D, which is why it is sometimes called the D. However, in the rules it is called the circle.

If the ball goes into the goal without otherwise leaving the circle, even if multiple defenders touch the ball after an attacker has touched the ball inside the circle, it is a score.

RUMOR RULE: Some people think the player who scores a goal should grab the ball and carry it up to the centerline. That is NOT a rule and should NOT be done, especially in games when time is stopped when a goal is scored. Immediately following a score, the ball is the responsibility of the team that was defending.

PLAYING THE BALL: Unless you're playing goalkeeper, you cannot use anything but your stick to move, stop, deflect, or otherwise play the ball.

The stick has a flat side and a round side. You can only play the ball with the flat side of the stick. The flat side includes the "edges" of the stick, which are the parts of the stick where the flat side and the round side come together. The round side of the stick is often called the back of the stick. Not even a goalkeeper is allowed to use the back of the stick to play the ball.

Only the goalkeepers (and field players with goalkeeping privileges) are allowed to kick the ball, but they only have that special permission while they are within 16 yards of the goal-line they are defending, i.e. when they are within their circle.

NO CONTACT: Field hockey is a non-contact sport. Incidental

contact isn't penalized but it is a breach of the rules to run into or push an opponent. If a player uses their body or stick to impede an opponent from reaching the ball, it is a breach of the rules called obstruction.

When a player attempts to get the ball away from an opponent (this action is called a tackle), the player must not contact the opponent or the opponent's stick (again, minor contact is not penalized). Even if they get the ball first, they cannot allow the momentum of their body or stick to contact the opponent. This is what makes collisions between a goalkeeper and an attacker tough calls for the umpire.

THE LINES: The ball must completely cross the sideline in order for the ball to be considered out-of-bounds, i.e. a ball on the sideline is inbounds. The ball must completely cross the goal-line in order for a goal to be scored. The goals are positioned just behind the goal line – they are not *on* the field of play. Therefore, in order to score, the ball must completely leave the field of play.

NOTE: The location of the player's body, inside or outside the lines, has no bearing on whether a ball is in or out. A player can be outside the field of play when defending or while in possession of the ball. An attacker's feet and the rest of their body can be outside the circle and they can score as long as the ball is inside the circle when they shoot. If any portion of the ball is above any portion of the circle line, the ball is inside the circle.

SAFETY: No one is allowed to play dangerously. Safety is the responsibility of the players. The umpires are responsible for penalizing dangerous and unsafe play. Umpires are asked to penalize a player with a ten-minute suspension if a defender knocks the ball carrier to the ground.

BALL OUT-OF-BOUNDS: When a ball goes all the way outside the sideline, it is out-of-bounds. The team that touched the ball last must defend a free hit from the point where the ball left the field. Things get a bit more complicated when the ball leaves the field over one of the backlines. When the defense touches the ball last, the attack begins from the 25-yard line or with a penalty corner if the defense intentionally played the ball over the backline. When the attack touches the ball last, the defense restarts play where the ball crossed the backline or up to 16-yards upfield and in line with where the ball went out.

PENALTIES: When a team breaks a rule, it is penalized by possession being awarded to the opponent and/or by having one or more of its players being suspended. The opponent is awarded a free hit or one of two penalty plays designed to give the team a scoring opportunity.

FREE HIT PROCEDURES: Players can "self-start" when awarded a free hit. In other words, players do not have to pass to a teammate when restarting play on a free hit (or when bringing the ball into play from a sideline). Part of the penalty is that the restarter is allowed an initial 5-yard buffer before opponents can try to get the ball or influence the play. Indirect-circle-entry (ICE) requirements, which are relatively complex, are applied for free hits taken by the attack inside the quarter of the field that their opponent is defending. Similar ICE requirements are applied to indoor hockey but for free hits taken by the attack inside the half of the court that their opponent is defending. Everytime a free hit is taken involving the ICE requirements, umpires have to make a dozen rule decisions as the ball is put into play.

How can you learn more? Begin by reading the rules!

The *Rules of Hockey* and the *Rules of Indoor Hockey* are available for free from FIH.ch.

Middle School Field Hockey Rules is available from Amazon.

An online umpiring and rules course is available on UmpireHockey.com.

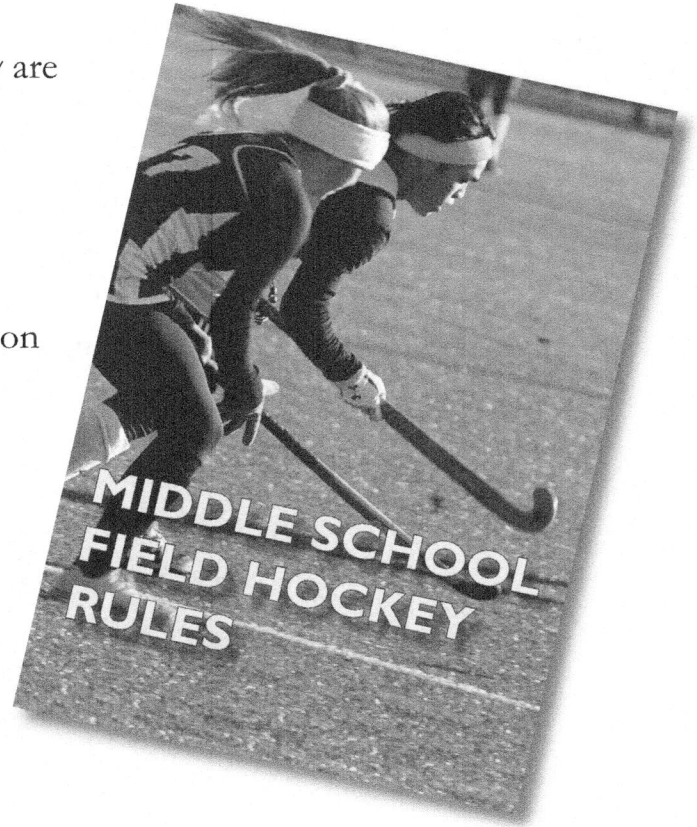

MIDDLE SCHOOL
FIELD HOCKEY
RULES

There are two special penalty plays in field hockey and indoor hockey, a penalty corner and a penalty stroke.

PENALTY STROKE: The penalty stroke is similar to a penalty kick in soccer. It is awarded when a defender illegally, even if by accident, prevents a goal from being scored or illegally and intentionally keeps an attacker away from a scoring opportunity. The award of a penalty stroke returns a scoring opportunity to the team that was fouled. A very high percentage of penalty strokes result in goals.

CHAPTER 8
PENALTY PLAYS

PENALTY STROKE

When a penalty stroke is called, time is stopped and the attacker places the ball 7-yards away from the center of the goal-line. A single attacker stands within playing distance of the ball but not closer to the goal than the ball. A single defender, almost always a goalkeeper, stands on the goal-line. One umpire stands behind and to the right side of the attacker and when that umpire is sure everyone is legally positioned and ready, they blow the whistle.

The attacker isn't allowed to hit the ball so they either push the ball along the ground or flick the ball into the air in an attempt to get the ball past the defender and across the goal-line.

PENALTY CORNER: The penalty corner is unique to field hockey and indoor hockey. It is awarded when a defender in the circle accidentally breaches the rules that wouldn't be "stroke worthy". It is also awarded when a defender intentionally breaches the rules outside the circle but in the section of the field containing the circle the opponent is attacking.

The award of a penalty corner provides an attacking advantage to the team that is fouled. Penalty corners often result in a goal being scored. How often? In international matches, the success rate is reportedly 25-35%, appoximately ten times more successful than other times the attacking team has possession in the circle.

In field hockey, only 5 players can defend the goal against the entire attacking team (as many as 11 players). An indoor penalty corner is different in that an entire team (all 6 players) can set

PENALTY CORNER

up to protect the goal, although only the goalkeeper can take up a starting position from within the goal. In fact, indoor hockey goalkeepers must start from inside the goal.

If time expires after the award and before the completion of either of these penalties, play is extended until either the penalty stroke or penalty corner in question is completed. Please refer to the current rules to learn all the different ways that these penalties end.

PENALTY PLAY ALTERNATIVE: When appropriate, options to the penalty corner and penalty strokes are possible. I'm fond of the Open Shootout, which can be used instead of a penalty stroke or penalty corner. This option is particularly helpful on fields without circle lines and in competitions when players have not yet learned the relatively complex penalty corner rules or the specialized individual skills used on penalty strokes.

A single attacker places the ball in the middle of the field, halfway between the goal-line and the center-line. The area between the goal and the ball is called the attacking quarter. A single defender is positioned inside the goal being attacked and all of the remaining players are in the other half of the field or court.

NOTE: If a goalkeeper is in the game for the defending team, the goalkeeper must defend the goal on an Open Shootout.

When all the players are ready, the umpire blows the whistle. At the sound of the whistle, all of the players can leave their positions and engage in open play.

Outdoors, the attacker can shoot only after moving the ball 5 meters. Indoors, the attacker can shoot only after moving the ball 3 meters.

If time expires after the award and before the completion of an Open Shootout, play is extended until it is completed. The Open Shootout is over when the ball goes out-of-bounds, leaves the attacking quarter, enters the goal, or a penalty is assessed that doesn't call for another Open Shootout or penalty stroke to be taken.

NOTE: The Open Shootout closely resembles the Challenge from Hockey5s, the game created by the FIH for use at the Youth Olympics.

Players who violate the rules can be suspended. This might happen because a rule was repeatedly breached or for a single blatant violation. Acts of violence, if seen by either umpire, will always cause the player to be suspended.

When a field hockey player is suspended, the umpire indicates a suspension by blowing the whistle to momentarily stop play and shows one of three different cards.

- **GREEN** (triangle): The athlete is suspended and the player's team plays with one less player for 2 minutes*

- **YELLOW** (square): The athlete is suspended and the player's team plays with one less player for a minimum of 5 minutes* (longer for violations involving violent acts)

- **RED** (circle): The athlete in question is expelled and the player's team plays short for the rest of the game

Interestingly, although the shape of the cards are not specified in the rules, only a green triangle, yellow square, and red circle

9
CHAPTER

SUSPENSIONS

INDOOR HOCKEY SUSPENSIONS
Green card = 1-minute maximum
Yellow card = 2-minute minimum
Red card = Expulsion

are viewed as being acceptable. It is said that shapes are used in addition to colors because eight percent of men are color blind and, therefore, shapes were employed to minimize misunderstandings regarding the level of suspension being given.

To suspend a player, the umpire blows their whistle, indicates which player(s) is being suspended, and shows the appropriate card. Suspended players leave the field without influencing ongoing play.

NOTE: In games between high schools in the USA, and only in USA high school games, the umpires are required to stop time when suspending a player.

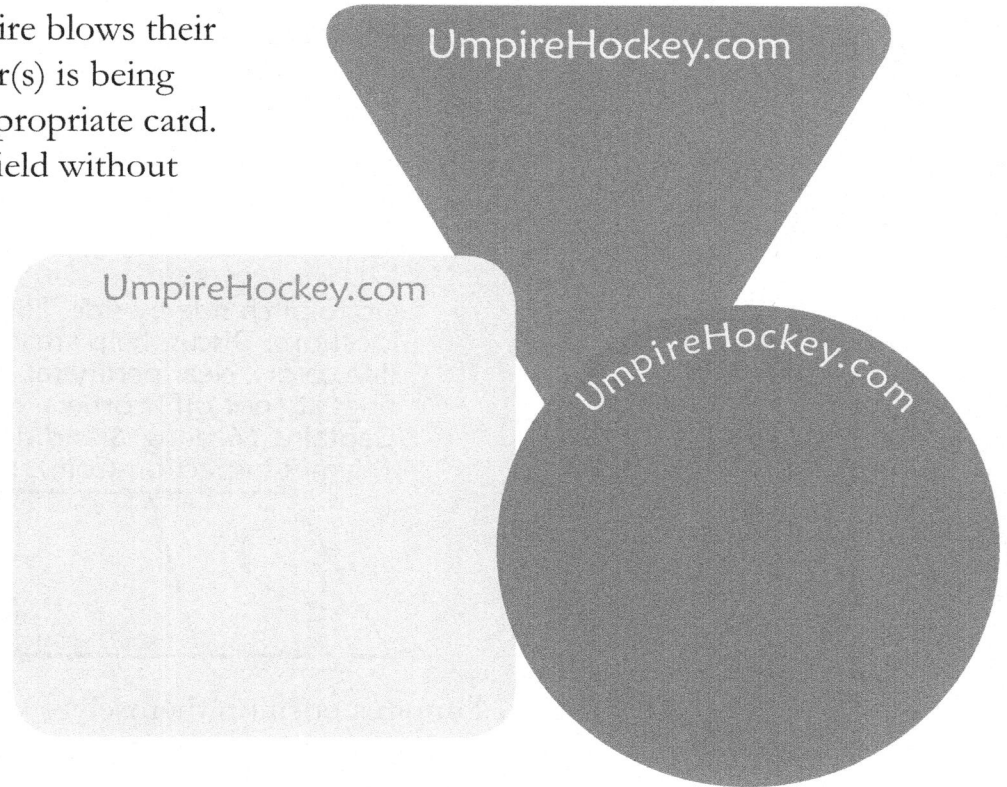

Two umpires, not referees or judges, officiate indoor hockey and field hockey matches. It is possible for one umpire to officiate small-format games.

The main jobs of the umpires, beyond enforcing the rules, are to keep things fair and to penalize dangerous play.

The umpires split the field on a diagonal as shown in the pre-game card from UmpireHockey.com.

10

THE UMPIRES

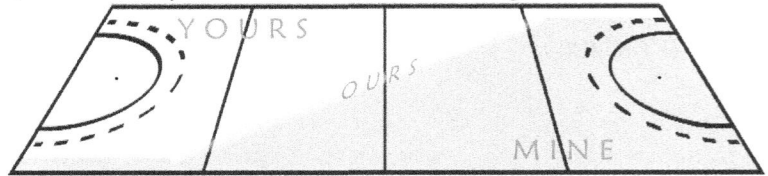

UmpireHockey.com Outdoor Pre-Game
Go to pitch side-by-side. Flip coin to determine umpire locations. Discuss help areas. Inspect markings, confirm line colors, clear perimeter. Ensure nets in good repair, flags at (not off) corners, cages at (not on) goal-line. Captains' Meeting: Stand side-by-side, use NIC process (Names-Inspection-Coin), max. length = 90 seconds.

Umpires position themselves with a good sight line to the athletes playing the ball and so they are relatively close to

the action. Separately, the umpires have sole responsibility for the circle and goal to their right.

Most umpires beyond play at the recreational level wear radios to enhance their ability to communicate with each other concerning game events.

Umpires use body language, their voice, a whistle, and suspension cards to "talk" to players during a game.

Umpires wear colored shirts and black pants, skirts, shorts, or skorts.

NOTE: Umpiring is a great way to earn money, exercise, make friends, and – perhaps – travel the world and represent your country in the Olympics. The teenagers in this photograph began umpiring when they were still playing in high school.

Being able to recognize the signals shown by umpires helps spectators, coaches, and players.

When an umpire stops play for a breach in their area, they blow their whistle and give the appropriate primary signal. When the ball goes out-of-bounds, signals are shown without a whistle being blown (unless the players appear to think that the ball is still in play).

There are two broad category of signals. Primary signals and secondary signals.

Primary signals are important. They are shown first and they tell the players what they have to do next, i.e. which way to go. Secondary signals are optional and they show the players what they did, i.e. what happened in the past.

Athletes seem to only care about primary signals. In fact, the only people who typically care about what happened in the past are the fans and coaches associated with the team being penalized.

If players demonstrate legitimate confusion about why a call was

11

UMPIRING
SIGNALS

made, especially when the result is a penalty corner or penalty stroke, the umpire should – if possible – show the appropriate secondary signal and/or verbalize the call to the players.

In all cases, whenever an umpire shows a secondary signal before the appropriate primary signal, that umpire is at fault for stalling the flow of the game.

ADVANTAGE: The advantage signal is shown to let everyone know that the umpire saw a breach but the umpire, rather than blowing the whistle, is waiting to see if the team going in the direction the umpire is pointing would be better off if play is allowed to continue. The arm pointing in the direction of the team that is to have possession of the ball, is held up in the air, well above shoulder height.

Notice that the umpire's hand is open— palm facing the players. Notice too that she is not reaching across her body. When her right arm is up, it will be the team attacking to the umpire's right that will get the ball if she blows the whistle. If her left arm were up, the team attacking to the umpire's left would get the ball if she were to have to blow the whistle.

46

DIRECTION (free hit): If the team attacking to the umpire's left commits a breach, and there is no advantage to award, the umpire will blow the whistle and show direction for the team attacking to the right. The signal is performed by holding the right arm up at shoulder height, parallel to the ground, and pointing towards the goal on the umpire's right.

As with the advantage signal, this umpire's palm is open, facing the players, and she is not reaching across her body. Good form is a sign of a well-trained umpire striving to make the direction in which the play should go easy for all the players (and fans) to see.

DIRECTION (free hit): When the team attacking to the umpire's right commits a breach, and there is no advantage to award, the umpire blows the whistle and signals that the team attacking to the left gets the ball. The signal is performed by holding up the left arm, shoulder height, parallel to the ground, and pointing toward the goal to the umpire's left. As noted on the previous page, the umpire would be pointing with the other arm if the situation were reversed.

As with the previous signals, this umpire's palm is open, facing the players, and she is not reaching across her body.

Field Hockey: The Beginner's Guide

DIRECTION (ball over sideline): When the ball crosses to the outside of one of the sidelines, the umpire – without blowing the whistle – holds up one arm, shoulder height, parallel to the ground, and points down at the sideline with the other arm. The arm that the umpire holds up is used to point at the goal that the team is attacking that didn't last touch the ball before it left the field of play. In the case of the situation shown in the photograph on this page, the team attacking to the umpire's right last touched the ball so she is pointing to the goal on her left.

If the ball were to be last touched by the other team, the umpire's arms would be reversed.

HIT IN DEFENSE: Another boundary ball is one that goes over either of the backlines. If a ball goes across a backline after it was last touched by the team that was attacking that end of the field, the umpire doesn't blow the whistle but holds both arms up, parallel with the backline. The palms of both hands are open and facing the centerline. This signal is commonly known as a "16" because the athlete restarting play can do so from as many as 16 yards away from the backline.

NOTE: If the defense last touches the ball before it crosses a backline, the umpire shows the direction signal to his right while indicating where the ball crossed the line.

STOP CLOCK: To tell the timekeeper to stop the game clock, umpires blow their whistle and cross their wrists above their head. The clock can be stopped by the umpire at their discretion, for example when there is an injury, lightning, or an animal comes onto the field. In some competitions, the team with the ball can ask the umpire to stop the clock to take a timeout. The palms of the both hands are open and facing the center of the field.

NOTE: The clock does not need to be stopped when issuing a penalty card (except, currently, in high school games played in the USA under NFHS rules).

PENALTY CORNER: When the defense accidentally breaches the rules inside the circle and the breach didn't impact a scoring play, the umpire blows the whistle and signals a penalty corner (PC). A PC is also awarded if the defense intentionally breaches the rules when the ball is outside the circle and within 25 yards of the backline (in indoor hockey, an intentional breach by the defense outside the circle but inside the half of the court the defense is defending is a PC). Another reason the umpire penalizes the defense with a PC is when the defense intentionally plays the ball over the backline. The umpire signals a PC by pointing both hands at the goal with arms extended and parallel to the ground.

PENALTY STROKE: When the defense intentionally breaches the rules inside the circle or when an accidental breach impacts a scoring play, the umpire blows the whistle and signals a penalty stroke. The umpire signals a penalty stroke by pointing one hand at the penalty stroke mark, which is 7 yards/6.4 meters from the center of the goal-line, with the other hand held high above the head. Timekeepers must stop the clock when this signal is shown.

NOTE: An umpire signaling a penalty corner or penalty stroke should give a secondary signal explaining what breach occurred (if there is one for the breach in question) because these penalties greatly increase the likelihood that a goal will be scored and everyone watching the game will want to know what happened.

SCORE: When a team scores, the umpire blows the whistle and points with both hands to the center of the field; arms parallel to the ground. The signal is consistent with telling the players what comes next and which way to go. With this signal the umpire is saying, *"A goal has been scored and I'm pointing to the center of the field because that is where play will restart."*

BULLY: The final, and probably rarest primary signal is to tell the players that play will restart with a bully. A bully is called when play is forced to stop and no breach of the rules occurred. There are two ways umpires signal a bully. One is to alternately move the hands up and down like a juggler at a carnival. The other, see photograph, is to mimic the bully action by alternately moving the hands up and down and touching them together.

HOW TO BULLY: The ball is placed between two opponents. The opponents face each other with the goal they're attacking to their left. The players place the heads of their sticks on the ground, on opposite sides of the ball. When the umpire whistles, the players touch their sticks above the ball and then try to get the ball!

Umpiring Signals

SECONDARY SIGNALS

Kicked ball

Stick obstruction

Body obstruction

Dangerous play

Obstruction by an offball teammate (cross and uncross arms)

Pushing (simulate pushing)

Encroachment

Back of Stick

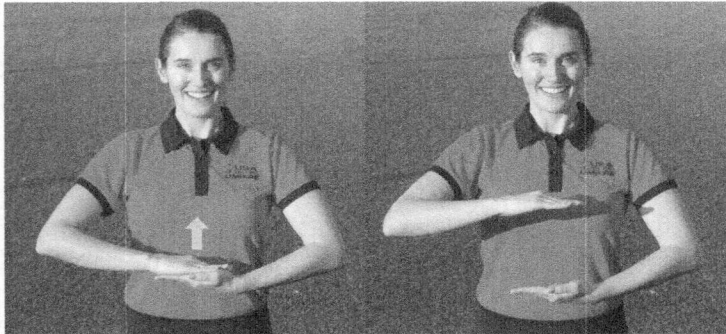

Illegally raised ball

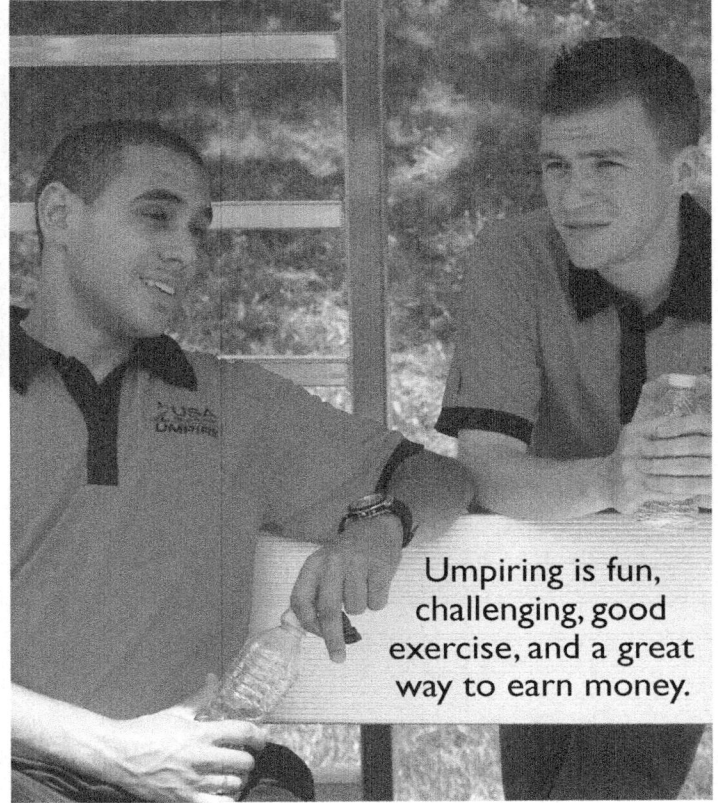

Umpiring is fun, challenging, good exercise, and a great way to earn money.

SPECIAL THANKS

(in order of appearance)

Thank you to Kelsey, Keely, Taylor, Kendall, Bian, Mina, Olivia, and Nick for their help in the umpiring section.

Umpires are needed for field hockey and indoor hockey. Start your training now by completing the online course. Learn more: **UmpireHockey.com/enroll**

CHAPTER **12**

MALONEY METHOD™: HISTORY AND BENEFITS

I first published what would later become known as the *Maloney Method™* during an International Olympic Committee *Olympic Solidarity* course in 1985.

The course was held at the US Olympic Training Center in Colorado Springs, Colorado, under the auspices of our National Olympic Committee.

The course director was Richard Aggiss, who was the head coach of the Australian Men's National Field Hockey Team at the time of the course. In fact, he was the head coach from 1981 to 1988.

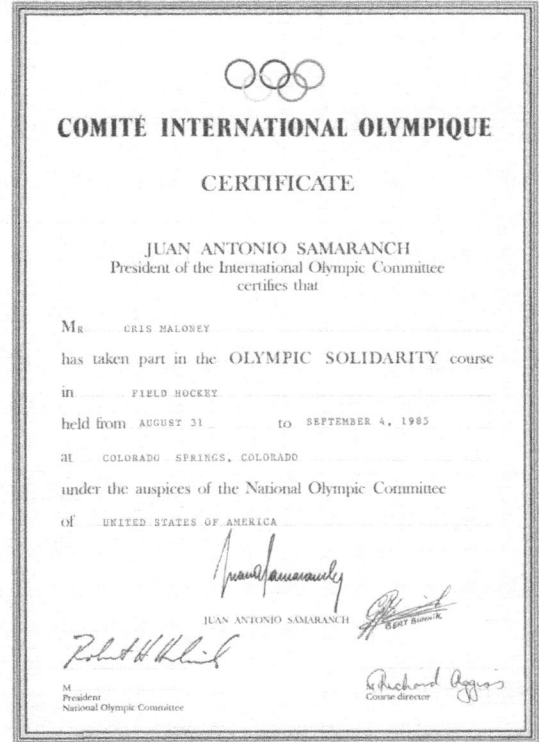

COMITÉ INTERNATIONAL OLYMPIQUE

CERTIFICATE

JUAN ANTONIO SAMARANCH
President of the International Olympic Committee
certifies that

Mr   CRIS MALONEY

has taken part in the OLYMPIC SOLIDARITY course

in   FIELD HOCKEY

held from AUGUST 31   to   SEPTEMBER 4, 1985

at   COLORADO SPRINGS, COLORADO

under the auspices of the National Olympic Committee

of   UNITED STATES OF AMERICA

JUAN ANTONIO SAMARANCH

BERT Búro-K

M
President
National Olympic Committee

Course director

My presentation at the *Olympic Solidarity* course was called *Field Hockey: The First 30-Minutes.*

Many attendees at the seminar thought I was going to talk about what a team's approach should be in the first 30-minutes of the game. They were surprised that, instead, I would cover what I thought were the most important things to do in a player's first 30-minutes with a hockey ball and stick.

By breaking down skills into easy-to-learn steps, supported by easily remembered key words and phrases, the *Maloney Method*™ helps athletes rapidly acquire the foundations of essential field hockey skills such as close-quarter ball control, dribbling, dodging, passing, and receiving.

Equally important in the development of the athletes, is the instructor's focus. The teacher has to immediately catch and correct the errors in each student's execution of the skills, repeatedly make those corrections, and insist on proper execution before moving on to more enjoyable activities where a beginner's imagination, experimentation, and exploration can take over.

The *Maloney Method*™, in as little as 30-minutes, will teach beginners about the stick, the three field hockey grips, how to hold the stick, how to control the ball, how to pass, how to receive, and – perhaps most importantly – how to dribble on the left and right sides of their bodies. By learning through the *Maloney Method*™, field hockey athletes can avoid the pitfalls that come with learning skills from well-meaning but poorly equipped coaches.

Said another way, by starting with the *Maloney Method*™, field hockey players can avoid having to unlearn bad habits.

Please note that the first ten steps of the *Maloney Method*™ can be completed in a little less than 30 minutes. Additionally, because the *Maloney Method*™ has well defined steps and is objective-based learning, it can be easily incorporated into a physical education unit on the sport of field hockey.

13

MALONEY METHOD™: GRIPS

Before we begin learning the steps in the *Maloney Method™*, we need to establish the grips that are used in field hockey and indoor hockey.

According to Wikipedia there are eight grips in tennis. They have fancy names like the Continental Grip, the Semi-Western Forehand Grip, and the Double-Handed Backhand Grip.

In field hockey, I have identified three grips and named them one, two, and three.

No matter what grip is used (in field hockey), the left hand is almost always at the top of the stick and always holds the stick in the same way.

The left hand, shown in the illustration, holds the stick firmly.

The right hand is relaxed and, with a

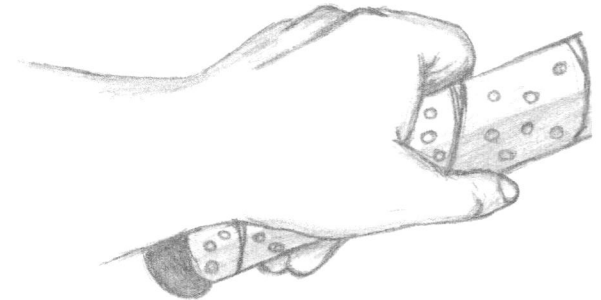

Field Hockey: The Beginner's Guide

position at about the middle of the stick, supports the weight of the stick. The right hand is not actually needed when learning the three grips.

If the left hand remains steady, one can tell which grip the player is using by which way the toe is pointing.

The different directions that the toe of the stick points when it is rotated in the left hand and associated grip names – 1, 2, and 3 – are presented below.

GRIP #1: This is the grip that we begin with when learning with the *Maloney Method*™. It is the most important grip because it is used to control the left "side" of the ball and to play the ball (backhand dribbling, passing, and receiving) when the ball is on the left side of the body. Defenders use Grip 1 to perform a tackle when an attacker tries to dribble to a defender's left.

NOTE: Not learning this grip would be like telling a right-handed basketball player not to learn dribbling with the left hand.

When holding the stick with Grip 1, the middle of the round side of the stick runs into the middle of the V formed by the left thumb and fingers. If the player extends their arm and looks down the stick, the toe of the stick points to the left.

An instructor can check the grips of a large group of players by having them face in the same direction and hold their sticks up in the air, perpendicular to the ground, with their left arms stretched out in front of their bodies. The toe of every stick being held with grip #1 will be pointing in the same direction – to the players' left. Looking at the players from the front, an instructor will see the flat side of all the sticks and the toes of all the properly held sticks will be pointing to the instructor's right.

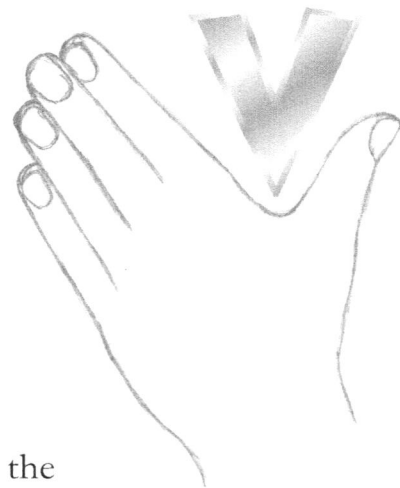

Maloney Method™: Grips

GRIP #2: During games, this grip is used more often than either of the other grips. It is natural and almost doesn't have to be taught (which is one reason it is so important to begin with Grip 1). It is, unfortunately, often referred to as the "handshake" grip. That doesn't make sense to me because it doesn't tell you which way the toe is pointing and suggests that the most important hand on the stick is the right hand – which is not correct.

Regardless, Grip 2 is used for controlling the right side of the ball and the back of the ball for forehand dribbling, passing, receiving, and shooting the ball when it is on the right side of the body. Defenders use Grip #2 to perform a tackle when an attacker tries to dribble to a defender's right.

When holding the stick with Grip 2, looking through the V and down the stick, the toe of the stick points up.

As with Grip 1, an instructor can check the grips of a large group of players all at the same time. The toes of all the sticks being held with Grip 2 will be pointing in the same direction – back over the heads – when the players hold the sticks up in front of their bodies.

GRIP #3: This grip puts the flat side of the stick up, away from the ground. Defenders use Grip 3 when they want to jab at the ball being dribbled by an attacker. Attackers use it for backhand edge hitting when the ball is on the left side of the body. The backhand edge hit skill is a very popular and exciting way to shoot on goal.

When holding the stick with Grip 3, the middle of the flat side of the stick runs into the middle of the V formed by the left thumb and fingers. When holding the stick with Grip #3, looking through the V and down the stick, the toe of the stick points to the right.

As with Grip 1 and Grip 2, an instructor can check the grips of a large group of players all at the same time. The toes of all the sticks being held with Grip 3 will be pointing in the same direction – to the players' right – when the players hold the sticks up in front of their bodies.

Grip 3 is used for skills that are taught <u>after</u> mastering the all-important foundational stick and ball control techniques covered in the next chapter.

To take players through the *Maloney Method™*, all the players need to have is a field hockey stick and ball.

With the stick and ball in their hands, have the players stand with their feet in the shape of a V – heels together, toes pointing out. You're ready to begin.

1. SADDLE UP: Tell the player(s) to place the hockey ball between their feet and "hug" the ball in position.

Holding the ball between the feet is especially important when beginning in a facility with hard flooring because it keeps the ball from rolling away. Tell the players that this is called the "saddle up" position.

Once they learn this basic position, the instructor can quickly collect a large group of players, each with their own ball, into a standard starting position by simply saying, *"Okay everyone. Please face this way and saddle up."*

CHAPTER **14**

MALONEY METHOD™: STEP-BY-STEP

In a gymnasium, where even a single hockey ball rolling on a hardwood floor makes a surprising amount of noise, saddling up helps quiet the room.

NOTE: *If the instructor reinforces this positioning a handful of times on the first day, the players will respond quickly to the instruction to saddle up in future lessons.*

As soon as the players have all saddled up, the instructor can teach them the parts of the stick. An objective for this part of the lesson is that the players should be able to identify the handle, the shaft, the head, and the toe.

2. TABLE (Grip 1): Have the players hold the hockey stick parallel to the ground and below their waist. The left hand is holding the stick by the handle, near the end of the stick. The handle is to the player's left and the toe is to the player's right. The right hand supports the head of the stick, the fingers under the shaft just before the stick begins to curve towards the toe.

Now is the time to look for and correct any issues with how the player holds the stick on the table.

If the arms are relaxed and extended, the flat side of the stick should be parallel to and facing the ground. If it isn't, the athlete's grip is wrong.

When the athlete has the stick on the table and the toe is pointing up, the athlete is using Grip 2. I describe the stick in this position as being "awake". When the toe is pointing down, I say the stick is "asleep" (the stick is being held imperfectly for the *Maloney Method*™).

In a matter of seconds, an instructor can check a large group of hockey players just by checking for the direction of the toes on their sticks while they have their sticks on the table.

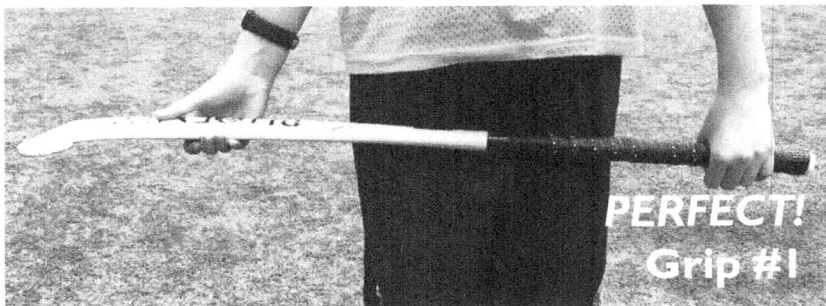

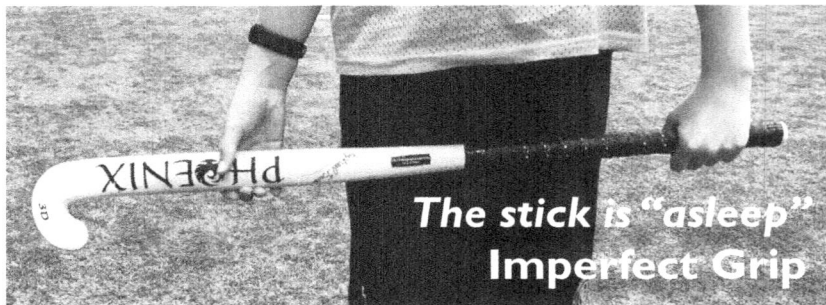

PERFECT!
Grip #1

The stick is "awake"
Grip #2

The stick is "asleep"
Imperfect Grip

70

INSTRUCTORS: I have found that with young players, it is best for the instructor to frequently stand with their back to the players in order for the players to more easily mimic the instructor's actions.

Players need to relax and straighten their arms. For some reason, perhaps because they're athletes, players seem to like to begin by holding the stick up by their chest instead of below their waist. I joke with beginners that they can have "lazy arms" when I see them holding the stick chest high.

INSTRUCTORS: It is important to make sure that the player's arms are straight and that the toe is not pointing up or down. Instead the toe is pointing away from the player, as if the stick is lying flat on a table.

3. SHINE YOUR SHOE (Grip 1):

When the players have the stick in Grip #1 and the stick is in proper position below the waist, the players "take away the table" (the right hand) and allow the toe end of the stick to fall so that the flat side of the toe ends up against the outside of the right foot.

INSTRUCTORS: To eliminate confusion, I have found that the instructor should demonstrate how the stick "falls" from the right hand and ends up on the side of the right foot.

The players should return the stick to the table and then take away the table three or four times. If the players are older than 9 years of age, they should be able to do this easily with only the left hand – moving the stick back and forth like a windshield wiper.

TIP: Moving the stick like a windshield wiper, using only one hand, is a good exercise for the wrist.

Field Hockey: The Beginner's Guide

With the stick off the table and down at the right foot, have the player – using the left hand only – rub the stick up and down on their foot. This is called "shining your shoe".

4. MAKE A RAINBOW (Grip 1): Looking down at their feet, with the flat side of the stick up against the right foot in shoe-shining position, the players – using the left hand only – make a rainbow by moving the stick from the right foot, crossing in front of their toes, and ending with the flat side of the stick on the outside of the left foot.

5. SHINE YOUR OTHER SHOE (Grip 1): With the flat side of the stick up against their left foot – and using the left hand only – the player rubs the stick up and down on their foot. Make sure the toe of the stick hits the heel of the left foot. As in the photograph on the right, the flat side of the stick should be visible from in front of the player.

Maloney Method™: Step-by-Step

Have the players move the stick back and forth, making a rainbow to the left and the right and back again. Players more than 9 years of age should be able to make rainbows easily with only their left hand. If a player is not strong enough to make rainbows with only their left hand, they can put their right hand at the end of the handle (just above the shaft) and use it to support the weight of the stick. This, however, can be problematic if the player holds onto the stick tightly with their right hand. The stick must be held firmly by the left hand but turn freely in right hand.

I have found that if a player cannot stop holding the stick tightly with their right hand, the problem can be fixed quickly by slipping the tube from the inside of a toilet paper roll down the handle stick and have the player hold the tube (and therefore the stick) with their right hand. Tell them not to crush tube!

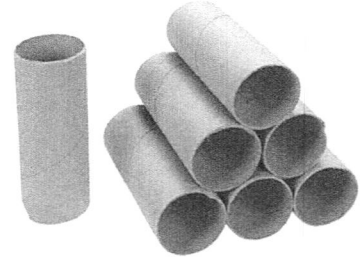

6. MAKE MANY RAINBOWS (Grip 1): The players should spend a few moments making many rainbows. The players should make sure that at the end of the rainbow from the right foot to the left, that the toe of the stick is brought into contact with their left heel.

INSTRUCTORS: Standing in front of a player, you should be able to see the flat side of the stick as the toe taps the left heel. It is very important that the players, before moving to step seven, perform this skill well.

Field Hockey: The Beginner's Guide

7. SHINE RIGHT SIDE OF BALL

(Grip 1): Now that the players are confident in controlling the stick, it is time to practice controlling the ball. To begin, the player takes one giant step backwards from the ball. With the ball directly in front of the player, the player takes up a comfortable stance with their feet a little more than shoulder width apart and knees slightly bent.

In a manner similar to shining the shoe, the athlete reaches out with the stick and shines the right side of the ball. All the players should use their right hand to support their stick. Remember, do not grasp the stick tightly with the right hand. It is next to impossible for a player to progress if they continue to hold on tightly with the right hand.

8. RAINBOW OVER THE BALL (Grip 1): After shining the right side of the ball, the player does a rainbow to the left side. Try to make the rainbow as small and tight to the ball as possible. Most players know the old saying that there is a pot of gold at the end of the rainbow. The players should dip the toe of their stick into that mythical pot of gold.

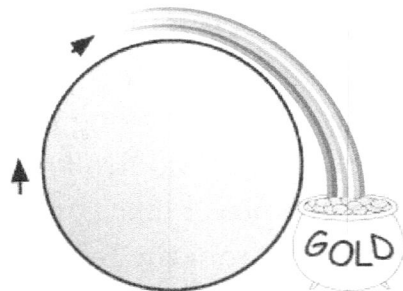

9. SHINE LEFT SIDE OF BALL (Grip 1): When the stick reaches the left side of the ball, it is critical that the tip of the toe hits the ground.

10. MAKE MANY TINY RAINBOWS (Grip 1): Players should spend a few moments making many tiny rainbows back and forth over and close to the ball. Perhaps a small challenge is to see how many tiny rainbows can be made in 15 or 30 seconds. Each time, the player must make sure to dip the toe of the stick into the pot of gold.

11. PUSH LEFT, PULL RIGHT (Grip 1): It's time to start moving the ball!

This action is commonly known as the "Yard Stick" skill. The players should saddle up, put the stick on the table, and step back from the ball. The players should take up a comfortable stance with their feet a little more than shoulder width apart and, again, knees slightly bent.

Reach out like before and put the stick on the right side of the ball. Staying in contact with the ball, push the ball to the left until it is just outside the left foot. Rainbow over the ball to the left side of the ball and pull the ball to the right until the ball is "home" outside of the right foot.

Rainbow back to the right side of the ball and begin to slowly repeat the pattern. The players might want to rock from side to side while rhythmically performing this skill.

The stick should stay in contact with the ball while it moves slowly back and forth. The rainbow action should be small and close to the ball as the push-rainbow-pull-rainbow-and-repeat pattern is mastered. Make sure the toe of the stick is dipping into the pot of gold!

Push | Begin Rainbow | End Rainbow | Pull

Maloney Method™: Step-by-Step

EXERCISE: The players should demonstrate that they are able to proficiently move the ball back and forth in front of them with control by accelerating the pace at which the ball completes the path from outside the right foot to outside the left foot and vice versa. The players should try to repeat each path at a faster and faster rate, counting how many times they can complete the paths in 15, 30, and 60 seconds. Each time a player pushes from the outside of their right foot to the outside of their left foot, they get a point. Each time a player pulls from the outside of their left foot back "home" to the outside of their right foot, they get a point.

NOTE: It is IMPOSSIBLE to get a high score when the player holds on to the stick tightly with their right hand. The stick must move freely in the right hand while the left hand holds the stick tightly.

The players should not try to go so fast that they constantly lose control of the ball and become frustrated. But, if a player never loses control of the ball, they are not trying to go faster than the level of skill they have already attained.

Pushing and pulling skills are the foundation of nearly every ball handling skill in the game.

12. WALK THE DOG (Grip 1 and Grip 2): Now it's time for the player to start moving the ball AND their feet! It is also the first time a grip other than Grip 1 will be used.

NOTE: Because "walking the dog" takes a little shoulder, arm, and wrist strength, this step should probably be skipped or modified for very young players.

At this point, the players have demonstrated that they can control the right and left sides of the ball. When "walking the dog" they will control the back and front sides of the ball.

1. To begin, the athlete should saddle up with the stick on the table

2. Take two sideways steps to the right of the dog, I mean, the ball
3. Place the stick at the back of the ball, be certain to maintain Grip 1

NOTE: Throughout the "walk the dog" steps, the left arm is stretched out, almost uncomfortably so, for the stick to reach the ball. The arm and stick are aligned, reaching out for the ball, creating (roughly) a 45 degree angle from the ground and their bodies. This position should not be a problem for players older than 9 years of age. Pretend that the ball is a dog...a very smelly dog. Therefore, the players want to keep their noses as far from the ball as possible.

4. Begin to "walk the dog" by keeping the

stick behind the ball and walking forward

5. At about 10 steps, or other marker, the players make a rainbow over the ball – to the front of the ball

6. Keeping the stick at the ball, the player turns to their left, taking a step closer to the ball, faces the starting point, and shifts to Grip 2. The stick and left arm are now crossing in front of the player. The ball is outside the player's right foot

7. The player adds their right hand in a support position low on their stick's handle and dribbles the dog home

8. Reaching home, the player shifts to Grip 1, makes a rainbow, stops the dog, turns to the right, and repeats the "walk the dog" drill until able to "run the dog" in both directions

Congratulations! The players have learned the most important foundational skills in field hockey using the *Maloney Method*™.

SPECIAL THANKS

Thank you Peyton, Raphael, Anna, and Coach Janice Axenroth for your help expertly demonstrating the steps used in the *Maloney Method*.

Thank you also to Centercourt Club & Sports, Lawrence Township, NJ, for the use of their weather-perfect facility.

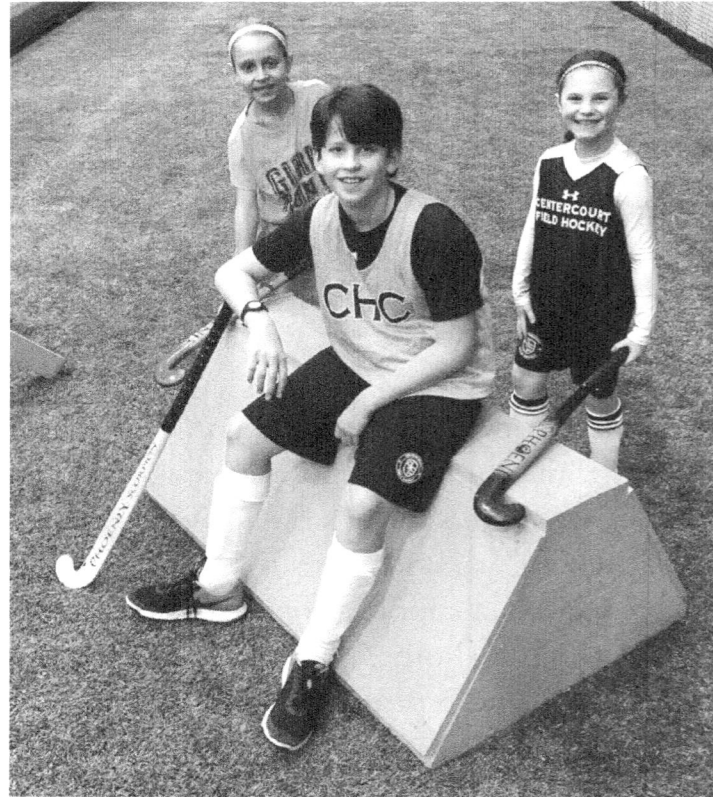

Field Hockey: The Beginner's Guide

CHAPTER 15

MALONEY METHOD™: TIPS FOR COACHES

My first tip is that coaches go through and practice the *Maloney Method*™ so using the 12 steps to introduce field hockey becomes second nature.

Learn the terms that were introduced to players as they were taken through the *Maloney Method*™ so you can use them as triggers to reinforce proper skills while players participate in drills, scrimmages, and games.

Here are some additional suggestions for coaches. These come from my 40+ years of teaching beginners and observing other coaches trying to do so:

- You'll see kids who should absolutely be playing the ball on their left side but don't make an attempt to do so. Maybe the ball is getting away from them on their left and they need to turn right to avoid going out-of-bounds. Shout out, *"Make a rainbow!"* If you see something like that but don't say anything, a moment later ask the player something like, *"What would have happened over there if you had used a rainbow?"* Learners like questions!

- When getting ready to receive a pass or play defense, many coaches yell, *"Put your stick down,"* but the ball still goes right under the player's position. What if the player takes the coach literally and drops their stick? Players will respond much better when coaches say something more precise and logical. I recommend, *"Put your hands below your knees."*

- When beginners are receiving their first passes, they often reach out their sticks in their eagerness to get the ball. Relative to the ball, the stick forms a ramp. When the ball reaches the stick, the ball pops up and either hits the player or goes beyond their position. Demonstrate how making a ramp with your stick, by reaching the toe of the stick out for the ball, makes it hard to stop the ball. Tell them that "ramping the ball" is actually an advanced skill that they should add to their game after they are more experienced. Show them how to trap the ball with their foot – heel down and toes up. Show them how to make this trapping position with their stick – toe of the stick near their feet, hands reaching far out in front of their body. Whenever you see the player ramping the ball in a drill or game, you can shout out a reminder, *"Hey! No ramps!"*

- It is natural for field hockey players to swing the stick from right to left across their bodies and pass the ball to their left. The bad news is that doing so sends the ball to the strong side of their opponent. Therefore, it is best for a player to go to their right, their opponent's weak side. The "go left" mistake is why beginners often get involved in a swatting match – the ball going back and forth between their sticks. For this reason, emphasize with beginners to go to their right, rather than going left only to end up smacking the ball back and forth with their opponent. Have two players face each other. They should both have a ball. Remind them of how they pushed and pulled the ball back and forth in front of their body in step 11 of the *Maloney Method™*. Have them do that now but after they push the ball to the left, do a rainbow, and pull the ball outside their right foot, another rainbow, and dribble the ball forward like taking the dog home. By doing this, the player will have dodged the defender by going right. Practicing going right with the illustrated "Rainbow Right" drill. It is a far better use of cones than having the players do a slalom down a line of cones that forces them to practicing going left. Once group drills and scrimmages commence, coaches should expect to constantly remind the players to, *"Rainbow right!"* Adding that, *"Right is right!"*

With the foundation set by using the *Maloney Method™*, players can move quickly to develop other basic skills, such as passing, receiving, dodging, and tackling. They can also begin to learn advanced skills, such as backhand edge hitting and 3D (off the ground) dribbling. Many of the individual skills that players can learn, are listed in Appendix 1, as part of the Skill Assessments.

Rainbow Right

Rainbow Right

Rainbow Right

16
NEXT STEPS

After mastering the basics presented in the *Maloney Method*™, what's next?

FIND PLACES TO COMPETE

Check with your township recreation department and/or school system. If field hockey isn't offered, work with them to start a program or have it introduced to the physical education curriculum. Teaching and learning field hockey isn't rocket science and with the *Maloney Method*™, you can help people start playing field hockey and/or indoor hockey very quickly.

Contact your national governing body. In the USA that would be USA Field Hockey (USAFieldHockey.com), to see if there is a club in your area that you can join. No club in your area? Start one!

Some national governing bodies have grants available to help people start a program in their area. At the time this book was written, USA Field Hockey, used a grant program it called FUNdamentals to provide local groups with free sticks, balls, cones, and a curriculum. Check to see if it is still being offered.

Individual skills will improve by dedicated exploration and experimentation. Use your imagination. Watch skill videos. Go to high-level competitions in your area, or watch broadcasts of those games, and copy what you see experienced players doing.

Practice individual skills, escalating the level of difficulty over time.

ENHANCE PHYSICAL AND MENTAL FITNESS

Engage in fitness and performance training. Field hockey athletes have to work on developing their endurance, speed, strength, and flexibility. And, working on physical fitness isn't the end of it. Field hockey athletes have to constantly make decisions about which way to go, what pass to make, how to receive a pass, how to get open for a pass, how to defend, when to fake, where to shoot, what save to make, remember personal conduct rules so they're not suspended, remember playing rules so they can restart play in a way that works to their team's best advantage, how to work with and encourage teammates, how to relax under pressure – to name just a few aspects of the mental fitness attributes needed to succeed.

IMPROVE TECHNICAL SKILLS

TechPitch™, created in The Netherlands by Albert Monpellier (Monpellier Sports Methods & Solutions, B.V.), is a training aid available in the USA from BolsterSports.com.

It can be unrolled in your house or at a practice facility. Athletes gain stick work skills, ball control (including 3D skills), and footwork by following skill patterns designed to help players excel. Use of the TechPitch™ helps cognitive development, strengthens neuromuscular pathways, and can be used during periods of rehabilitation.

One thing that is great about practicing on a TechPitch™ is its size. It forces players to make precise maneuvers.

Too many players practice dodges on wide open fields, performing what they think will be successful dodges in

games, only to find that when they do the same dodge in a game, they send the ball so far away from themselves and the player that they're dodging, that a different player from the other team is able to easily steal away the ball.

PERFORMANCE GOALS

Athletes should set and write down performance goals. Goals should be specific and measurable. For example, after an athlete practices and perfects a 3D maneuver on a TechPitch, they should write down the number of times they'll do a 3D dodge in their next game and then, strive to achieve that specific goal.

DON'T SPEND A LOT ON A STICK *(at first)*

Having a $300 stick will NOT make you a better player. In fact, skill performance will likely go down each time a player upgrades their stick. Each stick has a slightly different feel, different weight, handle thickness, center of gravity, and stiffness. More expensive sticks typically move the ball faster than less expensive sticks and when a player changes sticks they might not be able to stop the ball as well as before, passes might go astray, and they'll be more likely to lose ball control during dodges they had previously mastered. While these setbacks will be temporary, they help illustrate that a stick does not a hockey player make – practice does.

There is no reason for young beginners to spend much more than $50 to $60 for a new field hockey stick. Players would be served well by having a goal to completely wear out their stick before they get a new one. All sticks will quickly gather scratches, chips, or other minor imperfections. A stick that is truly worn out has structural damage underneath the surface. A player who invests their time and energy in skill development, fitness, rules knowledge, and setting goals – and not their money on "another new stick" – will be better than any lazy player with the most expensive stick on the planet.

APPENDIX **A**

SKILL
ASSESSMENTS

Listed in the skill assessment tables are all the skills covered in *Field Hockey: The Beginner's Guide* and some additional skills including:

- Pushing the ball along the ground and into the air

- Receiving a ball along the ground on the forehand and backhand sides

- Receiving a hip-high ball on the forehand and backhand sides

- Forehand and backhand sweep hitting the ball along the ground and into the air

- Dodging (dribbling past an opponent without losing ball possession)

- Tackling (taking a ball away from an opponent)

Instructional videos for a nearly unlimited number of the skills used in field hockey and indoor hockey can be found online.

Feel free to photocopy and distribute the assessment pages.

SKILLS ASSESSMENTS

	ALWAYS / VERY GOOD	OFTEN / ACCEPTABLE	NEVER / WEAK
MALONEY METHOD™ ....Name Stick Parts	☐	☐	☐
MALONEY METHOD™ .... Saddle Up	☐	☐	☐
MALONEY METHOD™ .... Stick on Table	☐	☐	☐
MALONEY METHOD™ ....Shine Right Side of Right Shoe	☐	☐	☐
MALONEY METHOD™ .... Rainbow, End with Stick to Heel	☐	☐	☐
MALONEY METHOD™ ....Shine Left Side of Left Shoe	☐	☐	☐
MALONEY METHOD™ ....Shine Right Side of Ball	☐	☐	☐
MALONEY METHOD™ .... Rainbow over Ball	☐	☐	☐
MALONEY METHOD™ .... Shine Left Side of Ball	☐	☐	☐
MALONEY METHOD™ .... Walk the Dog	☐	☐	☐
MALONEY METHOD™ ....Take the Dog Home	☐	☐	☐

SKILLS ASSESSMENTS (continued)

	ALWAYS / VERY GOOD	OFTEN / ACCEPTABLE	NEVER / WEAK
BALL CONTROL ....U12 Yard Stick (60 times per minute)	☐	☐	☐
BALL CONTROL ....U14 Yard Stick (75 times per minute)	☐	☐	☐
BALL CONTROL ....U16 Yard Stick (90 times per minute)	☐	☐	☐
BALL CONTROL ....U19 Yard Stick (100 times per minute)	☐	☐	☐
BALL CONTROL ....U21 Yard Stick (120 times per minute)	☐	☐	☐
PUSH/FLICK....................Push the ball from a Stationary Position	☐	☐	☐
HIT...............Forehand Sweep the ball from a Stationary Position	☐	☐	☐
HIT...............Backhand Sweep the ball from a Stationary Position	☐	☐	☐
DRIBBLE........................Run To and Dribble Away a Stationary Ball	☐	☐	☐
HIT.......................... Run To and Forehand Sweep a Stationary Ball	☐	☐	☐
HIT.......................... Run To and Backhand Sweep a Stationary Ball	☐	☐	☐

SKILLS ASSESSMENTS (continued)

	ALWAYS / VERY GOOD	OFTEN / ACCEPTABLE	NEVER / WEAK
PUSH/FLICK............Lift ball ~18 inches from Stationary Position	☐	☐	☐
HIT........................Raised Forehand Sweep a Stationary Ball	☐	☐	☐
HIT........................Raised Backhand Sweep a Stationary Ball	☐	☐	☐
PUSH...Push the ball from a Dribble	☐	☐	☐
HIT..Forehand Sweep from a Dribble	☐	☐	☐
HIT..Backhand Sweep from a Dribble	☐	☐	☐
PUSH/FLICK................................Lift ball ~18 inches from a Dribble	☐	☐	☐
HIT........................Raised Forehand Sweep from a Dribble	☐	☐	☐
HIT........................Raised Backhand Sweep from a Dribble	☐	☐	☐
RECEIVE...........Using Forehand Ground Ball (no bobble)	☐	☐	☐
RECEIVE...........Using Backhand Ground Ball (no bobble)	☐	☐	☐

SKILLS ASSESSMENTS (continued)

	ALWAYS / VERY GOOD	OFTEN / ACCEPTABLE	NEVER / WEAK
RECEIVE.........Forehand Hip-High Ball (drop to playing position)	☐	☐	☐
RECEIVE........ Backhand Hip-High Ball (drop to playing position)	☐	☐	☐
DODGE.................Rainbow, Pull Right, Rainbow, and Push to Go	☐	☐	☐
DODGE..Push Left, Rainbow, and Pull to Go	☐	☐	☐
TACKLE..Retreating Jab	☐	☐	☐
TACKLE...Forehand Block	☐	☐	☐
TACKLE..Backhand Block	☐	☐	☐
TACKLE...From Behind (toe up, right to left)	☐	☐	☐
TACKLE..............................From Behind (flat side up, left to right)	☐	☐	☐
DEFEND .... Move to Left and Approach Attacker	☐	☐	☐
DEFEND ....Channel Attacker by Shadowing Their Movements	☐	☐	☐

SKILLS ASSESSMENTS (continued)

	ALWAYS / VERY GOOD	OFTEN / ACCEPTABLE	NEVER / WEAK
DRIBBLE/BALL CONTROL............................Air Dribble 25 Times	☐	☐	☐
DRIBBLE...90^0: Close Control for Time (Left)	☐	☐	☐
DRIBBLE.......................................90^0: Close Control for Time (Right)	☐	☐	☐
DRIBBLE.......................................180^0: Close Control for Time (Left)	☐	☐	☐
DRIBBLE.......................................180^0: Close Control for Time (Right)	☐	☐	☐
DRIBBLE.................Maloney Agility: Close Control for Time (Left)	☐	☐	☐
DRIBBLE...............Maloney Agility: Close Control for Time (Right)	☐	☐	☐
TechPitch™ ....Number Zero (Forehand and Backhand)	☐	☐	☐
TechPitch™ ....Numbers 1 - 9 (West and East)	☐	☐	☐
TechPitch™ ....Small Square and Big Square	☐	☐	☐
TechPitch™ ....Small Triangle and Big Triangle	☐	☐	☐

SETUP (90°, 180°, AND MALONEY AGILITY)

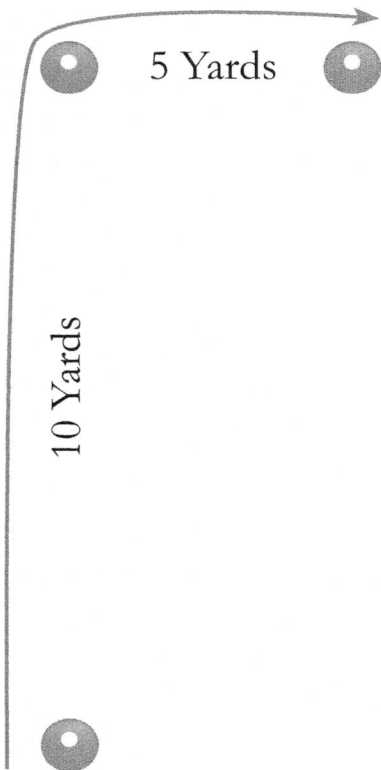

5 Yards

10 Yards

90° Turn Right

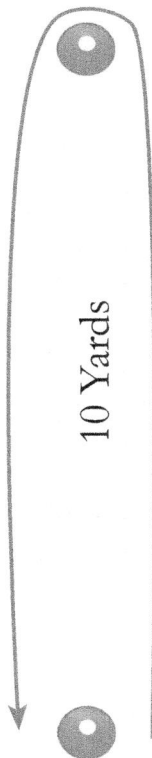

10 Yards

180° Turn Left

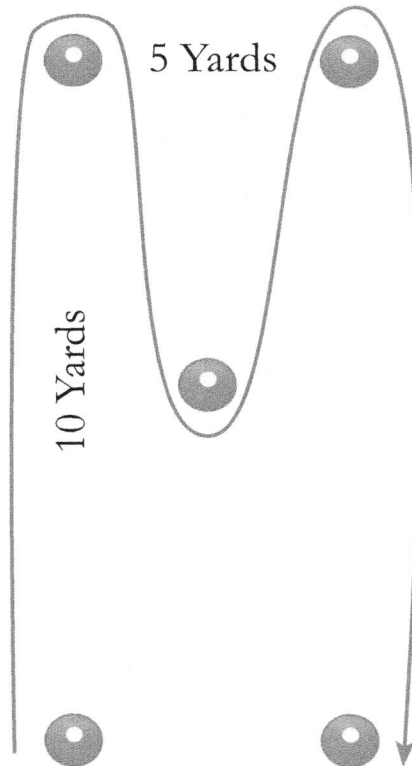

5 Yards

10 Yards

Maloney Agility – Right

This page is from *Field Hockey: The Beginner's Guide,* available from Amazon.

BolsterSports.com

Field hockey products for schools, clubs, players, coaches, and umpires.

FIH.ch

The International Hockey Federation (FIH) is recognized by the International Olympic Committee as the international governing body for field hockey.

UmpireHockey.com

Home of the online *High-Performance Umpiring & Rules*™ course, the official training course for multiple umpire associations and taken by students in twenty-one US states and five countries

USAFieldHockey.com

USA Field Hockey is recognized by the USA Olympic Committee and International Hockey Federation as the national governing body for field hockey and indoor hockey in the USA. No matter what country you play, coach, or officiate in, join your national association!

ABOUT THE AUTHOR

Cris Maloney is the author of *Field Hockey: Understanding the Game, JUMP IN! A Beginner's Guide To Field Hockey Umpiring, Middle School Field Hockey Rules*, and *Field Hockey: The Beginner's Guide*.

Maloney began playing field hockey while in college, after success in track at Moorestown High School, Moorestown, NJ (he was a 1975 All American). He became a nationally certified field hockey umpire in 1977.

In the 1980s, Maloney founded New Jersey's Garden State Games Field Hockey Event, served as an assistant coach to two undefeated, gold medal field hockey teams in United States Olympic Committee national sports festivals, attended an *Olympic Solidarity* coaching seminar offered by the International Olympic Committee where he presented his paper titled *Field Hockey: The First 30-Minutes*, the catalyst for the *Maloney Method™*. It was also when he began doing play-by-play announcing at international games. Later he became a nationally certified Level II Umpire Coach.

Always an innovator, in 2003 Maloney was the first field hockey assigner to use web-based technology to assign umpires to field hockey games. He was the first, in 2005, to use, recommend, and supervise umpires using walkie talkies during high school games. In 2013, he organized the first Hockey5s league in the USA. In 2014, he created a version of field hockey called Super6s— which is a combination of the indoor and outdoor games that favors simplified rules and continuous action. Super6s can be played by children and adults and easily umpired by new umpires.

Maloney is the owner of BolsterSports.com, produces an online rules course, and gives presentations to groups of teams, coaches, and umpires. He runs field hockey programs for boys and girls in central New Jersey.

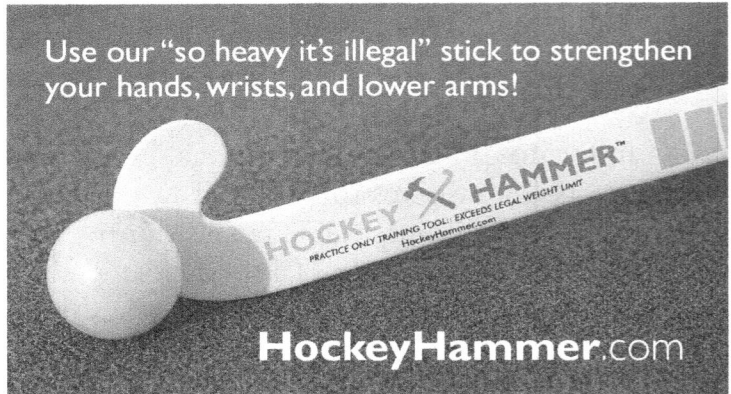

Made in the USA
Middletown, DE
01 June 2021